CONQUER STRESS AND LIVE AN ANXIETY FREE LIFESTYLE

LIVING WITHOUT NEGATIVE HABITS AND OVERCOMING EMOTIONAL STRESS

JONATHAN GREEN

Edited by
ALICE FOGLIATA

CONTENTS

DON'T GO IT ALONE

The hardest part of dealing with stress is going it alone. When you are in isolation, the night can seem so dark. Please join my FREE, private Facebook group filled with supportive people on the same path.

https://servenomaster.com/tribal

THE HEART ATTACK

I woke up early that Monday morning with an unbelievable pain in my chest. I felt like something was ripping through my ribcage; my heart felt like it was melting through my chest at a thousand degrees, burning my bones. I did not think I was going to live another hour, let alone another day. As we rushed to the emergency room, I could not think of anything other than the fact that at thirty years old, I was not ready to die. Too soon, too young; how could this happen to me?

When I arrived at the emergency room, there was a large crowd there. The nurse took one look at me and put me straight to the head of the line. When the doctor came in and began running his tests, I saw fear in his eyes – the last thing you want to see when you are in a hospital. If you are on a plane and things get bumpy, as long as the stewardess is not scared, you know that everything is going to be okay, but when you see that look of fear in her eyes or, even worse, she starts crying or praying, that is when you know you are really in trouble.

When I saw the doctor looked nervous, I started to get even more scared. Maybe it was too late, and he could not help me. When the doctor walked out of the room, I wondered if they were going to send in a priest. My entire mortality passed before my eyes, all because of a sneak attack by the silent killer: stress.

After that morning, I decided that I needed to change my life forever. I needed to do whatever it took to excise stress for my life, and I needed to change the way I approached business, relationships, health, and everything else. My entire life became dedicated to minimizing stress because thirty is far too young to die from something so stupid.

WHERE THIS BOOK WILL TAKE YOU

This is a simple book with a simple promise; I am going to teach you how to minimize the stress in your life. By the time you finish reading this book, you will be able to isolate, understand, respond to and overcome the causes of stress in your life. If you have read one of my books before, you know how these journeys go. I am going to share with you many personal stories about how I ended up in that emergency room and how I managed to walk out again, and I am still here ticking seven years later.

Whether your doctor has already warned you about stress or not, it is a major component of your life. If you have noticed other areas of your life where stress is affecting you, then we need to take action together, and we need to be very serious about this. I will lead by example and show you how I transitioned my life; I will share the steps you can take to break through the most powerful and dangerous force on the planet today.

CREATE A JOURNAL

This is a cooperative book. It is not a book full of trite sayings and cute lines you can memorize. This is a book of action, and I would like you to join me on this journey.

Get a notebook: it is going to be your Conquer Stress Journal. If you prefer, you can use a computer file instead. I'm a big believer in physical notebooks; I like writing my notes out by hand, but if you are listening to an audiobook and taking notes on your phone, you have that option too. Just find a way to take notes as you work through the activities.

It's tempting to read a book, especially on an e-reader, and take no action. We make promises to ourselves that we will take notes later or highlight our favorite sections. But be honest with yourself. How many books have you read this way and forgotten just a few days later?

This book only works if you take action, and the first step is to participate in this process fully.

1

LET'S TALK ABOUT STRESS, BABY

Before we go any further, we need to understand what stress is and how we are going to solve it. If my definition of stress is different than yours, then my solution will not fix your problem. We want to be sure that our language means the same thing. You may have noticed, if you watch the news, that two different people with opposing political views can use the same word with completely different meanings.

To avoid any confusion, let me dial into what I mean when I talk about stress. Stress is persistent anxiety; it is where your fight-or-flight response is activated in the long term. If you spent six weeks wondering if you are about to get downsized, the fight-or-flight reflex pumps a bunch of chemicals into your body that are designed to prepare you for combat and survival. Just like when you turbocharge your car by turning on the nitrous (if you are a street racer or have ever seen a *The Fast and the Furious* movie) – it is bad to do it all the time.

Your fight-or-flight reflex is meant for emergencies. If you keep yourself in a constant state of alertness, readiness falters. We cannot stay in a constant state of fight-or-flight, or we die. Something that is good for a moment is not good for weeks, months and years on end.

Imagine a submarine that stays at red alert for weeks on end. The constant stress and alertness causes the submariners to lose focus. They can't sleep, as they are constantly expecting an attack. If you are feeling persistent stress, your body is turning into that submarine.

There are loads of causes of stress in modern society, and they can come from all the things around us. Stress is the main way that other people leverage us into doing what they want us to do. If you have a boss, your boss will use stress to control you. When you're a child, your parents use the same technique to keep you from going out at night or doing dangerous things.

Earlier today, I caught my daughter drinking water from a public pool – the same public pool that my son pooped in three days ago. I know that little kids swim in that pool all the time, and it is at best half water and half urine, but something tells me it is closer to eighty percent urine. When she drinks that water, she gets sick, and when she gets sick, she cannot swim for a week or two. I explained this to her using fear, which is a precursor to stress; things we're afraid of cause stress.

On top of that, I placed a punishment structure in place; I said, "Every time I catch you drinking water in the pool, you immediately have to stop swimming. You get out of the pool and back into the house." This is me using stress to protect her; I do not want her getting fecal bacteria into her body and bloodstream.

As we get older, more and more layers of stress are piled upon us until we feel like we are walking through life carrying a backpack filled with sand. When I was in high school, you had two groups of people; you had the people who wore a backpack on one shoulder and had at most one book or one magazine in there, and then you had the super nerds who would fill their backpacks up with what seemed like dozens of books, and they would be hunched over.

I had a friend who used to carry so many books in his bag it damaged his back, and he had to have surgery to correct it. You do not want to go through life like that, with a backpack filled with unnecessary books. You only need the books for your next class in your bag; you do not need the books for the entire day. Going back to your locker is not that big of a deal; that is why it is there.

I believe that the worst invention to ever touch mankind is the clock, and it only got worse when we developed the wristwatch. The wristwatch is what turned us into slaves because now people can tell us that we are late; they can say, "Hey, I told you to meet me at a specific time," and this is where we began to experience stress. The advent of the watch coincided with a massive spike in loads of diseases, and today, stress is the number one killer in America.

Most people do not know that because they do not realize how many diseases are caused by stress; everything from diabetes to heart attack to strokes and loads of other maladies can be caused by it. If you look at the top ten medical causes of death in the United States every year, at least six of them are directly or indirectly caused by stress. If you lower the stress level in your life, you will live longer, and you will live better. Stress is the opposite of freedom, and I am a big believer in freedom; it is the thing I value the most, and it is what I want to give to you.

In other books, I have talked a great deal about achieving financial and emotional freedom; now it is time to achieve another layer freedom and to break off another set of chains that society uses to control us. There a lot of other causes of stress that are a little more sinister because they are subtle; for example, you might be stressed because of conflict between people you care about, such as your friends and family, or because of an illness affecting you or your or someone you love.

When you are a caregiver, when you have difficulties at work, when you do not have the education, training or finances that you need, when you lose your job, or when you have a lack of self-confidence – all of these situations cause stress. If you turn on the news on top of all that, it will be a competition to see who can stress you out more.

Local news every day around lunchtime will start their ads for the six o'clock news, trying to get you to watch them instead of the other channels. They will say stuff like, "Something your house is trying to kill you; find out at six!" Then I have to spend the six hours between now and then wondering if there is a killer in my house. They do this every single day, and this is why people who watch the news and get really engaged in them start to act weird. They are in a constant state of stress.

We see this more and more in our culture and around the world; people become obsessed with the news and need to know everything, and yet, all it does is kill them. The news is designed to use stress against you, to get you to come back day after day to find out what is happening next.

We always hear that the economy is about to collapse, we are about to go to war, and the environment is about to kill us. My entire life, the government has been telling me that the environment was going to kill me. When I was a child, first they told me that the ozone layer was going to develop a hole because of the Styrofoam wrappers for McDonald's burgers, which would eventually cause a big enough hole to allow all the radiations for the sun to come in and end all life on earth.

Styrofoam was developed by one of the largest companies in the world, and their patent was about to run out in the mid-eighties. With the patent running out, this company launched a disinformation campaign to convince the world that we were all going to die from holes in the ozone layer mainly because they wanted to continue to make money by selling their new replacement technology. If we take the time to research the things we are afraid of, we will often find that it is all about money.

After the scare about the hole in the ozone layer, which I have not heard about in thirty years now, there was the fear of acid rain. It was the idea that the atmosphere was so toxic that when it rained, the water would hit your skin and burn it off. This was about twenty-five years ago, or the early 1990s, and since then we have moved on to a whole new batch of fears to keep us in line.

The government and news media kept coming up with other ideas to continue to keep us stressed out; one of them was spontaneous combustion. It seems ridiculous now, but we used to hear about it all the time. Basically, the idea was that you might just explode. Our bodies are almost completely made up of water, and water is very hard to detonate. The idea of someone spontaneously combusting is ridiculous because it is scientifically impossible.

We go from fear to fear, and of course, we have some new ones today. First was global cooling, and now there is global warming. Not many people know that the same person came up with both theories and wrote books about them. Global warming is big business; a vice-president made a PowerPoint presentation and went from being one of the poorest former politicians to a billionaire. Loads of people love that movie and never considered that he made a cool billion dollars with that scare tactic. Whether he is right or wrong, whether the information is true or false, whether you believe in global warming or not, I can tell you this; within five years, they will have another scare for us.

They come up with new ones all the time, and of course, we live in a stressful world. How could you not be stressed when you are told that there are millions of things out there that could kill you at any time? The news, politics, and the world around us are very stressful, before we even start to deal with our own lives. If you engage with people who make a living from selling stress, it does not matter if it is true or false; their job is to get you engaged.

Modern websites are all about getting the click, and they want to say the most extreme things they can without getting in trouble. This is why they violate people's privacy and write things that are absolutely ridiculous; it gets the click, and if you visit their webpage they make a few pennies. They will say whatever it takes, no matter how dastardly or untrue.

It is possible that I have already stressed you out with the start of this book. I brought these things up only so that together we can eliminate them from your life. We are going to go through a powerful process to eliminate all of these, and I would like to start with a simple exercise.

Exercise One: Create your Conquer Stress Journal

Grab yourself a nice one-dollar journal or a spiral notebook and write on the top of it in big letters: Conquer Stress Journal. You are going to use this as the tool to change your life. This is an interactive book; we need to do physical things if we want to change our lives and make a difference. If you write something down, you are far more likely to remember it.

As we go through our exercises and stress-relief techniques and delve into how you are feeling at certain points throughout this book, if you do not write it down, in a few weeks you will not remember your answers, and you won't be able to measure your trajectory. With a journal, you will be able to see your progress, your improvement, or how you are feeling better. In order to make a difference, you are going to have to be a little bit proactive.

Now that you have your Conquer Stress Journal, the first thing you are going to do is to write down the causes of stress in your life; what makes you feel stressed out? What really gets to you and affects the way you feel? Maybe it is money, maybe it is politics or news, maybe it is your children – whatever is causing you stress, if we want to defeat it or overcome it, we have to understand it. We are establishing a baseline.

The biggest causes of stress in my life come from my children and finances. It is unbelievable how expensive kids are; they constantly need new things, whether it is school bills, toys they have broken, or medical bills. I just cannot believe how much baby stuff costs; a chair for myself cost about ten percent of what a chair for my infant costs. But what are you going to do? Baby stores know they have you over a barrel; you are not going to buy a discount high chair that might collapse with your child in it. Products are overpriced to take advantage of your stress; it is fear pricing, isn't it? I buy a more expensive high chair because of the fear of my son getting hurt if I try to save a few bucks.

Reflection Questions

Please write the answers the following questions in your Conquer Stress Journal:

1. Did you find anything surprising in this chapter? Why?
2. Now that you know you are working with someone who was on the same path as you and that it is possible to lower your stress levels, do you feel more empowered? Do you feel a greater sense of encouragement? Do you feel like you can finally see that first peak of light at the end of the night when it shows dawn is coming?
3. What are the biggest causes of stress in your life and how are they affecting you?
4. How much of a problem is anxiety in your life right now?
5. Do you think there might be causes of stress in your life you have not yet identified or noticed, that you are not even aware of yet?
6. Do you feel like there are any sources of unnecessary stress in your life? Extra stress that is there for no reason and no purpose? Take a moment and reflect on what you could do to eliminate those unnecessary and extraneous cause of stress.
7. Do you think keeping a Conquer Stress Journal will be helpful to you? If you are not sure about it or you do not like putting in the effort, think of ways that you could make the Journal more helpful for you. You can add in your own elements if you wish. This is why I encourage you to use your notebook, so that you can add your own sections.

2

HOW PREVALENT IS STRESS IN YOUR LIFE?

We have started talking about the big picture but now let us dial into the small picture and focus on just you, because you are all that matters. This book is about you and me, and from here on, it is all about helping you. I would like you to answer a few short questions to analyze where you stand on the stress spectrum. Are you someone who just has the occasional flare-up or a little bit of anxiety? Or are you someone who is living in a constant state of shivering, sweating, horror, and covered in terror sweat? Please answer the following questions, give yourself a score at the end of the quiz, and I will see you in the next section.

Test

1. How often would you describe yourself as "stressed out?"
    a) Very often, or often.
    b) Very rarely, or once in a while.

2. How often do you feel anxious as a result of life circumstances?
    a) Often, or very often.

b) Very rarely.

3. Do you ever worry about situations in which you might panic and make a fool of yourself?
    a) Very often, or often.
    b) Very rarely, or once in a while.

4. Do you ever overreact due to a temporary lack of self-control and focus or because you feel overwhelmed and helpless?
    a) Sometimes, or often.
    b) Very rarely, or once in a while.

5. Do you ever feel that you have nothing to look forward to?
    a) Most of the time, or often.
    b) Very rarely.

6. Do you find it difficult to relax and calm down?
    a) Yes.
    b) No.

7. Do you ever feel scared without being able to identify any good reason?
    a) Sometimes, or often.
    b) Very rarely, or once in a while.

SCORING: THE MORE "A" answers you chose, the more likely it is that stress is very prevalent in your life.

Exercise Two: Stressor Analysis

In the previous chapter, we did our best to isolate and find the biggest causes of stress in your life. Now we are going to go one step further; pick one of those causes of stress and answer the following questions:

1. Why is this stressor present in your life?
2. Why is it so strong in your life?
3. Do you think there is anything you could do right now to weaken the influence of this stressor?
4. Do you think this cause of stress is necessary in your life? Is there a way that you could completely eliminate it from your life? Why or why not?
5. If you feel like the stressor is unnecessary and could be eliminated from your life, why have you not done it yet? What has held you back? Why do you feel you have subjected yourself to this unnecessary and extraneous cause of stress?
6. What negative effects has this stress had on your life? What have the negative effects been on your health, relationships, happiness, business, career, and life?

Discussion

Now it is time for some free-form writing in your Journal. If I still have not convinced you to use a journal, that is unfortunate, but I understand. Please, at least take the time to have a short mental discussion with yourself about each of these questions. Do not promise you are going to answer later or come back later, as we both know that is a lie; don't lie to yourself.

I want you to experience change, and these exercises and activities are about more than just reading through them; they do not work if that is all you do. Please take some time to analyze these discussions and feel free to write out an entire section in your Journal for each of these.

Exercise Three: Three Sources of Stress

Choose three more of the largest cause of your stress and brainstorm ways you can diminish their impact or begin to remove them from your life. What are some ways you could decrease these causes of stress or at least decrease their impact on your body? Feel free to go wild with your imagination and be creative; it is okay to think outside the box. That is often where we find our best solutions.

The Workplace and Stress

One of the most common sources of stress is the workplace. We have developed a world and a culture that is constantly shoving more and more stress down our throats. Most of us in the West have shifted from one career to career families. We now need two people working full-time jobs in order to maintain our homes. Homes have gotten massively more expensive; they take you thirty years to pay off.

Some people do not like to hear this, but study after study has found that equality in the workplace has significantly increased stress amongst women, and women across the board experience lower levels of happiness then they did before. This is not to say that I am against equality; this is simply to say that people are less happy now and more stressed.

Women used to live much longer than men but now, courtesy of having the same careers and the same stresses, they are dying sooner. That is horrible. The workplace is a killer, and you would not even be there if it was not for stress. If you did not need to pay the bills, you would not go to work.

I know plenty of people who inherited loads of money, and they do not take work very seriously because they do not have to. It is almost like a hobby for them; when your parents can loan you a million whenever you need it to try a new business idea, it is a different experience than when you are wondering which bill to pay this month. Should you pay the health insurance or the electric bill? That is stressful!

The workplace is the source of so many causes of stress because we live in a constant state of flux. Your boss uses fear and hope to control you. You are trapped in a constant state in between the fear of losing your job and the hope of getting a raise. A successful boss will keep you trapped right between these two magnetic poles so that you are constantly stuck in a state of low-level stress; you want to make more money, but you are afraid to ask for it because you think that if you ask you might lose your job, and the money you are making now is better than making no money at all. That is an absolute nightmare, and I have been down that cycle myself.

I started working for myself after the last time I got fired, shortly before my massive heart incident, because I was tired of being in a situation where someone else could control my income streams, my life, and my health.

I did not fully learn my lesson, otherwise I would not have had my massive hospital experience just a few months later. My life had to get worse before it got better. Starting to work for myself was not nearly enough, lest you think quitting your job and starting your own business is the answer at the end of this book. It is not nearly enough to eliminate stress in your life. Believe me; this book is more than just some trite answers.

Exercise Four: Workplace-Related Stress

Let us take a few moments and think about your workplace-related stress. What are the causes of stress in your work environment? They are not always about money; sometimes it is about having a bad boss or working with someone who is incompetent. It is pretty much every experience I have ever had of a boss, and I wonder if my employees feel the same way about me. Hopefully they do not!

Maybe it is your coworkers, maybe you have someone who takes credit for your work, or you have one of those bosses that say things like, "If you do not come in on Saturday, do not bother coming on Monday." There are plenty of bosses, especially mid-level managers, who are dedicated to getting you to work extra hours so that they can work less. They want you working Saturday and Sunday, so they can spend Friday afternoon playing golf instead of working, and on Monday morning they can show up and take credit for your work.

I know we all wish this were just a silly plot line for movies, but unfortunately, art imitates life. Maybe you have a coworker who makes you feel uncomfortable or unsafe. While I have not experienced a boss asking me for intimacy in exchange for a promotion, I have experienced a coworker nearly choking me out while I was at work. We experience horrible situations in different ways.

I want you to think about your workplace stress and think about ways you can eliminate or begin to diminish it. I am starting off by putting the emphasis on you coming up with ideas before I start giving you loads of my ideas. I am trying to teach you how to fish rather than just hand you a single fish because new causes of stress will come in your life as you conquer old ones. Learning this ability is very important for the long term. I do not want you to have to re-read this book every three months.

When my coworker nearly killed me, I was initially afraid, and then I realized, "Wait a minute, we're not in high school!" I went and complained to my manager. I was working in a very large company, and they realized very quickly that I could sue them for putting me in an unsafe work environment. What is the point of all the key cards and security guards if another coworker can get physical with me? Looking back, they should have fired my coworker, but they just moved him to another shift in another department, and I never saw him again. For me, the problem was solved, and that was good enough. I eliminated one cause of stress in my life.

There is one critical thing that I want to dial into before we close off this chapter. The way we react to stress determines how much it can affect us. Sometimes, things happen in life that affect us in a major way; they get our blood boiling and our pulse racing, and this can influence us significantly.

Sometimes, something similar happens, and we just do not care. If you can become like the willow, that is when you are truly powerful. When there is a powerful storm, whether it is a tornado or a hurricane, strong trees with hard trunks resist, resist, and then they snap. It is the trees with the flexibility of a willow that bends in the high winds, and when the wind stops, they snap back up, and they are fine. They can endure more stress than those that we think are strong at first.

A lot of our society misunderstands the true meaning of strength. If you can learn to go with the flow and just accept the things that happen, which means changing how you react to them, then the power of that stress becomes diminished. This is just the beginning of our journey; I have a great deal more to share with you. I cannot wait to meet you in the next chapter.

NEGATIVE REACTIONS TO STRESS

As we've already touched upon, many of us tend to react to stress in negative ways that actually make the effect of the stress worse.

One of the things that can result when we use such negative reactions is the creation of high anxiety levels. Remember that stress and anxiety are not the same things, and our reactions to stress can either lessen or amplify the effect that stress has on us, including our levels of anxiety.

We often hear the word "anxiety" in our daily lives, but what exactly is it? A general definition of anxiety is a consistent feeling of fear, nervousness, worry, and/or unease in response to some kind of uncertainty.

Below is a list of some common negative reactions to stress. As you read them, think carefully about whether any of them apply to you. If any of them apply to you, think about how severely they apply to you.

Something that all of these negative reactions have in common is that they tend to make your stress level worse. This is despite the fact that these negative habits fool us into thinking they are helping on a temporary level.

Bad Habits

Stress is one of those problems that manages to magnify itself. When we are stressed out, we can enter cycles where we do things that make our stress stronger and stronger. We have these negative behaviors that serve to create more and more stress. They are often stress-coping mechanisms, but the way we deal with stress actually makes the problem worse.

There is a host of different ways you can get sucked down that path; I would like to share quite a few of them with you. Maybe some of these will be familiar, or maybe you are early enough in your stress problem that some of these have not entered your life yet.

1. **Smoking.** Everyone knows smoking is bad for you. There are still few doctors out there who will claim that smoking is not bad or is even good for you, but if you take a quick look, their studies are always paid for by tobacco companies, so no one trusts them anymore. We all know what is going on there, and yet people still smoke all the time.

One of the big reasons we smoke is that we are stressed out; I smoked for a long time. Whenever I was feeling anxiety or was stressed out by a project, I would have a smoke break. Taking a break is fine, but the problem is that in many workplaces, they will not let us take a break. If you say, "Can I have a fifteen-minute break?" they will not let you, but if you pull out a cigarette and go outside, they will give you that break no questions asked. It is one of the advantages of being a smoker.

While there is a benefit to taking a little break, the negative effects of smoking outweigh them. Sometimes, we feel a short jolt of a good feeling when we have a cigarette; we feel relaxed, we get those chemicals, and that nicotine feels good.

The stronger the addiction, the more we crave that feeling – that miniature high where we start to feel a little bit relaxed. If we smoke enough, eventually, we even start our day with a cigarette; smoking becomes the first thing we do in the morning.

There are loads of reasons why smoking is bad for you, and we know that in the long term, it can destroy your health. Smoking is bad for your lungs and your heart and arteries; it is bad for your entire internal system. It is connected to loads of diseases, and you smell terrible. The amazing thing about smoking is that the only person who does not know how bad you smell is the smoker.

It is also a very expensive habit. You will notice that the price of cigarettes is constantly going up, and it is all due to taxes. The government is trying to do the same thing with sugar now. The mindset is that you should not do it, and if you do, you should be punished. Smoking can start to eat away at your income stream. You are stressed about your job because you do not have enough money, and yet your smoking habit is eating away a lot of your income.

2. Drinking. At first, you start to feel good, and your problems start to disappear as your memory fades away, but when you wake up in the morning, and the hangover is kicking in, you feel terrible. You pay a heavy tax when you drink too much. Alcoholism is a total nightmare – it destroys families, relationships, and careers. I have dealt with it in my family. It is one of the most common reasons to drive people to homelessness.

When you have too much stress at work, sometimes you just want to make it go away. That is where phrases like "drink the pain away" or "drown my sorrows" are used to justify the habit. We down that alcohol in the hopes of lowering stress, and it works for a little while. But the problem is that stress starts to build up behind that wave, and the only way to keep it away is to start drinking more, until we are drunk all time. Otherwise, it is only a short-term fix for a long-term problem.

Again, drinking destroys your health, on top of everything else. While it feels okay for today, it makes your problems worse in nearly every single category tomorrow. You start drinking because you are stressed about your job, and then drinking starts to affect your relationship with your spouse, so you have a new source of stress, and you drink even more to deal with the second source of stress, and the problem compounds itself; this is how stress works.

When we have a negative response to stress, we do things that make it worse; they make the problem bigger, and we get stuck.

3. Comfort eating. We are all looking for a different type of fix in our society, and there are plenty of people who eat too much to cope with stress. We have a huge number of people in America that are obese; people who are way too heavy because they eat too much.

Obesity shortens your lifespan; there is a direct correlation between waist size and how early you die. We know it is bad for us, and yet we cannot seem to stop ourselves; it is a response to stress, and it is not a good one. "I had a bad day at work, but at least the food is here for me." Some people in our society have this new culture of almost idolizing food and talking about how even though the opposite sex or maybe the same sex isn't interested in us, food always treats us just the way we want to be treated. People have begun to personify their snacks. If a bag of chips started talking to me, I would be horrified, not excited.

We get caught up in this loop, but we all know that there is no health benefit to being overweight; it always shortens your life. Think of every fat comedian you have ever liked; they always die young. If someone is overweight though, we cannot tell them that something is killing them because it might hurt their feelings. We are developing a strange culture where we are not allowed to say it anymore. In our society, we have decided it is worse to hurt your feelings than it is to let you die early. Feelings have become more important than survival.

It is so easy to get caught up in a food cycle; you start to feel bad about yourself, so you eat more. If you have ever wondered how some people get trapped in their homes and eventually trapped in their beds, they go through these cycles where they feel worse and worse to the point where they do not care. This is how someone can get up to seven hundred, eight hundred or even a thousand pounds. Of course, you never see one of those people in their seventies or eighties. They never live that long.

Some of us deal with stress by eating too much, and we live in a society where it is easy to get access to too much food.

4. Fasting. Sometimes, to deal with stress, we go in the opposite direction: "I am too stressed out to eat." We can go too far in the other direction and enter cycles that cause us problems with our weight in the opposite way. We get too thin, we are not eating healthy, and we get underweight.

People can end up on a cycle of eating comfort food, fasting, eating comfort food, and then fasting again. It is a very unhealthy lifestyle. Especially if we feel like food is the cause of our stress, sometimes we opt for short-term starvation.

You might not be familiar with this technique as it is not nearly as common as comfort eating, but when you go through long periods of fasting, it limits your body and mental function. It can even start to cause mental problems or side-effects such as insomnia. Your body does not have enough of the right vitamins, minerals, and chemicals it needs to operate properly, and you start to operate less and less efficiently. You need the right chemicals to keep the machine running.

5. Compulsive spending. More and more we hear the phrase "retail therapy." I was recently watching a movie featuring the Brat Pack of the late nineteen eighties called *St. Elmo's Fire*. One of the characters was spending and maxing out credit cards so she could live the life she wanted. When she lost her job, she was so stressed out that she just started spending more. Eventually, she was pushed to the edge and nearly killed herself when the repo team came and took everything away. If people could control their spending, we would not have repossession in our society.

We live in a culture where we buy things that we want now – only to pay for them later, and we often end up paying ten, twenty or thirty percent extra just to do that. We get stuck in these cycles, and while retail therapy might make you feel good in the short term, study after study shows that the fix lasts for a very short amount of time.

No matter how expensive the purchase, after about two weeks, it starts to lose its luster. You buy yourself that ninety-thousand-dollar car, and you will feel really good when everyone is checking it out in the parking lot. After about two weeks, it is no longer special; it goes from a new purchase to an old purchase. If we want to stay ahead of the game, we have to buy something all the time. This is why so many people lease their cars.

Everyone knows that leasing a car is a terrible financial decision and a bad way to spend your money. The return on investment is very low on cars, and yet people do it all the time because they know they need that new fix, and they keep shortening the lease period – five years, three years, two years.

Pretty soon, you get into a cycle where you are just paying a massive amount of money to rent a new car every month so you can get that fix, but you will never get ahead of it. While you are doing this, you are creating a new source of stress in your life where all that money used to be.

6. Overconsumption of caffeine. Just like people who smoke talk about how many packs a day they smoke, there are loads of people on a cycle where they discuss how many cups of coffee they drink a day.

Coffee is also becoming increasingly grotesque and overindulgent in America. It is filled with caramel, extra sugar, and extra flavors, so now it is also making you fatter while caffeine is messing with your heartbeat.

We do it to stay alert, and it becomes another addictive habit. Caffeine is the most addictive substance in the world. There are several studies confirming that it is massively addictive; it messes with your brain chemistry. When people wake up in the morning and need a cup of coffee to start their day, it is not because caffeine wakes them up; it is actually a response to the addiction. We are no longer trying to wake up; we are trying to get back to normal.

Caffeine provides a short-term burst of energy, but it is only temporary, and it disappears soon. If you have too much caffeine, it will blow your heart right out of your chest. Wait to see what happens when you drink too many energy drinks; it will send you straight to the emergency room. There is a reason I do not drink energy drinks anymore, and it involves my own trip to the emergency room.

When I had too much stress and was working too much, I was pounding them because I wanted to work longer hours. It made my problem worse; it compounded everything instead of making it better. With all these fixes, we get a short-term solution that increases and magnifies our long-term problem.

7. Driving too fast. When we are feeling stressed out, sometimes we get behind the wheel and imagine going two hundred miles an hour like in those movies about street racing, and we start driving faster and faster. It feels pretty good, but of course, you are creating a danger for yourself and everyone around you. You are also increasing the chances of you getting pulled over and in trouble with the police. Or something even worse.

8. Overusing tranquilizers. This can manifest in many ways. Just like caffeine brings us up, we use tranquilizers to help us calm down. Sometimes, we take a sleeping pill at night because we are so amped up from all of the caffeine we drank during the day that we cannot get to sleep. If you have anxiety or panic attacks or too much stress, your doctor might prescribe you tranquilizers, but when we hear about someone taking too much medication and killing themselves, it's often sleeping pills and tranquilizers.

Reflection Questions

Like all of the other reflection questions activities in this book, please use your Conquer Stress Journal to write down your answers, so that you have a permanent record of what we have shared and what you have accomplished. Please answer the following questions:

1. Which of the negative reactions to stress do you recognize yourself practicing? If you do not relate to any of the ones listed in this chapter, are there any other negative reactions to stress that you tend to experience?
2. Is there anything that was not on this list that you know you are doing and it is not good for you? Please describe it and explain why it is negative.

Reflect on your plan for reducing your dependence on negative coping mechanisms and reflect on why it is important to start making those changes now.

4
───────

DEALING WITH STRESS IN A POSITIVE WAY

A s we've already learned, we have control over the way we react to our stress. And the way we choose to react to our stress can determine how much or little the stress affects us.

In chapter three, we talked about negative ways of dealing with stress. These were coping mechanisms people use that actually make their stress level worse and create new sources of stress too.

In this chapter, we will discuss positive ways of reacting to stress. These methods are positive because they help to lessen the effect of stress on you, but also because they are generally good for you.

Below is a list of examples of positive ways to respond to and deal with stress.

Positive Ways to React to Stress

I do not want you to get down in the dumps after reading the previous chapter and thinking about all of the bad things that stress can do to you. A dangerous aspect of stress is that the more we think about it, the worse it gets. It can turn into a new double worry, "I am so stressed I am starting to worry about my stress."

Last year, I went to take a physical at the hospital. I sat there, looking at the blood pressure machine and thinking, "Oh my gosh, I really do not want to have super high blood pressure. I am so afraid my blood pressure is a problem; what if that happens to me?" I had just written a book on diabetes, so these medical problems were in my mind, and I knew how devastating it can be.

Staring at the blood pressure machine, I made myself so nervous that my score skyrocketed and in fact, at the end of my exam, they wanted to put me on the very medications that I know destroy your life and rip you to pieces. Once you are on them, it is nearly impossible to get off them.

Fortunately, I said, "Let's run the test again," and this time I did not look at the numbers. I relaxed and received a much better score. I now own a blood pressure machine, and I check my numbers nearly every day (at least once a week), and my numbers are very close to perfect. We can increase our stress and make the problem worse by thinking about it; instead of responding negatively, let us go over a few positive ways that we can react to stress.

1. **Meditation.** There are many ways to practice meditation, and if you have been following me for a while or have read some other books, you already know that I teach a great deal about different aspects of yoga and meditation to achieve inner peace. We can disconnect, the process of meditation from any religious aspects.

Meditation has a physical value in that it allows you to relax your mind and remove all the things that are stressing you out. The beauty of meditation is that it clears your mind. We often spend a great deal of mental bandwidth on negative thoughts that are causing us problems.

The average person can think about five to seven things at a time. If two or three of those are stressful thoughts, taking some time to meditate and cleansing your palate will remove all those little stressful things that are in the back of our minds, and we might not even be aware of.

The beauty of meditation is that it helps you to strengthen your thought control, and you get used to controlling what you think about and what you actively choose to not think about. When those stressful thoughts slip through your mind, you can go, "Hey, you do not belong here. Get out of town."

2. A hobby that you enjoy. I have a great deal of hobbies. I like everything from artistic to sporty hobbies; video games, surf, paddleboard, kayak, swimming with my family, and I enjoy designing and coloring books. All these hobbies relax my mind and fill my time with something that is not stressful. Leisure time has a huge value.

Our bodies are designed to include leisurely activities; if you work twenty-four hours a day, you will not live very long. If you wake up, work all day, go to sleep, wake up, work all day, go to sleep, eventually, your system will collapse, starting with your mind.

Leisure activities have nothing to do with being lazy; on the contrary, they help to reset your mind and strengthen yourself. If you want to become a master weightlifter, you do not go to the gym and do the same exercises every day for fourteen hours; your body will never get stronger that way. Bodybuilders and weightlifters use an entire strategy for how much they work on each part of the body, which exercises they do, and the cycle and schedule they use; when they are training, they ensure that they have proper rest periods in between each exercise. We want to do the same thing with our lives.

I have designed multiple coloring books and written books about the power of coloring books because they are a very effective tool. With a coloring book, you can make it as difficult as you want; you could start off with crayons, work your way up to colored pencils and even oil paints, which are very complicated and require a great deal of focus, both in terms of technique and staying within the lines.

You can continue to improve and strengthen the power of distraction. You cannot concentrate on stressful thoughts when you are doing something that requires all your focus. It is very hard for me to surf and think about something stressful at the same time. I have to think about each part of the process, especially when I am trying to catch a wave. It only takes a few seconds of distraction to miss a wave and wipe out.

Find an enjoyable activity that takes up a lot of your mental bandwidth and strengthens one of the other areas of your life and personality, whether it is your creativity, your artistic side, or your physical side and health. Even activities that replenish your sense of spirituality are wonderful ways to enjoy a hobby.

3. Exercising. This flows in with building a hobby. I find that if I do not exercise for more than forty-eight hours, my stress levels start to skyrocket. There is a direct correlation between physical health and your stress which can be easily measured in blood pressure.

Your blood pressure can be a measure of your current stress levels; whether you eat poorly, skip exercise or whether you are just stressed out, all these things raise your blood pressure. It is a number worth tracking; I track it regularly to see if there are areas of my life where I am letting things slack off.

Exercise is great because it releases special chemicals and hormones into your body that lower your stress levels and help to heal the damage caused by too much stress.

4. Listen to music. It is very important to pay attention to what you are listening to. If you listen to angry music, you will become angry; if you listen to stressful music, you become stressed out. I cycle through different types of music; sometimes I want to accelerate a mood, and sometimes I want to reverse a mood. If you are feeling stressed out, it is not the right time to listen to heavy metal or any type of music that accelerates that mood; you want to listen to music that pushes you in the opposite direction. This is a great time to listen to Yanni or Portishead; classical music or trip hop are what I listen to when I am feeling stressed out or I want to push my stress down.

You might not be a fan of trip hop, so find the genres that help you relax. I have music I listen to that increases my anger and my energy; when you are playing a video game, and you have got to shoot a whole bunch of zombies, then heavy metal is the right music. Find tunes that help you relax; this can be a very beneficial addition to your stress-reduction strategy.

5. Go to a movie. Just like dealing with depression, dealing with stress does not have to be hard; it is supposed to be fun! The opposite of stress is fun, so do things that are pleasurable and enjoyable for you. I have a friend who cannot go to the movies because all he does is sit there thinking about work; movies do not work for him. They work for most people though, and they certainly work for me.

It is very different to go to the movie theater than it is to watch one at home. Going to the movies is very relaxing, especially if you are in a movie that fully engages your attention. If you are like my friend and don't enjoy movies, you can find other things to fill your time. It does not necessarily have to be a movie; there are other things that you can just add in your life that are not enough to be a full hobby. You can go to the arcade, play miniature golf or drive those tiny cars you can drive around on the racetrack. Anything that takes time and focus but is enjoyable and a little treat at the same time.

6. Read a book. Reading a book or even listening to an audiobook can be very relaxing. The type of book you read will make a big difference. Find books that are relaxing for you.

There are certain books that I cannot read. I recently grabbed an audiobook about vampires, and I thought, "This could be pretty cool." Honestly, it was too scary for me, and I had to stop listening to it. I have to admit that with you; sometimes I like to read a thriller, but if a serial killer book is too scary, I end up paranoid all the time. The mood of the book affects me, and that is why I mostly read books about space. I do not like books that are too close to home either. I like space adventures that take place at least a thousand light years away.

Find books that are relaxing and pleasurable for you. While it is good to read non-fiction books, and I appreciate that you're reading this book, that is often not the same as relaxing; for instance, this book entails a little bit of work because I am teaching you some methods. Intersperse this with something that is purely reading for pleasure.

7. Spend time with your friends. As humans, we are social creatures, and we need to spend time with other people to reset and recalibrate where we are mentally. Connecting with other people helps us to push away stress, as stress works in isolation.

When you are with your friends, you do not need to spend all your time talking about your problem, even though sometimes we feel like that is the best thing to do. "Ah, I wish I could have a release valve and get everything out there." Sometimes, talking about the same thing over and over again just makes it worse.

Last week, I was drinking with someone who kept telling the same story about a girlfriend he had broken up with six months before; I left pretty soon. I did not terminate my friendship with the person, but I do not want to sit and listen to the same story over and over again. When you are releasing your stress, be conscious of the people around you. If all you are doing is putting poison into the time you spend together, no one will want to spend time with you. If you have a little bit of stress, you are allowed to get it out once, but then you want to move beyond it. The best thing to do with your friends doing activities that are fun together.

8. Find a sport. Sport is different from exercise; with sports you have scorekeeping, winning, and losing, and that separates it from pure exercise. Running is exercise; the only way to win at running is to be faster, but there is not enough to it.

Soccer (or football) is mostly about running, but you have a ball, and you are trying to kick it in the other team's net; there is a scoring element, and that adds a whole new dimension to it. A game is different from a toy for the same reason; a toy is something to play with, while a game is something you can win or lose.

The brilliance of doing something where there are points, and you can win or lose is that it activates a different part of your brain, and it involves a different way of interacting with other people. If you are lifting weights next to somebody, all you can do is compare who can lift more. there can be a little bit of competition, but it might activate a negative part of your competitive nature, "I have got to beat this guy."

We want to go beyond that because we are trying to conquer a very specific problem that can manifest itself within your body. The real key here is that sports are fun. Find something that is physical and uses up your energy but you enjoy. The more of your spare time you spend having fun, the more effective every other element of this process becomes.

9. Sit in the garden. Sometimes, spending a little time with nature is exactly what we need to recharge our batteries and reset our internal feelings. I am a big fan of waterfalls.

Connecting with nature is part of how we were designed; our bodies were designed and perfected in a world where we are in contact with nature all the time. Sometimes, just sitting in the garden or going to the park can be incredibly helpful. When I was living in the States, I used to go to national parks all the time. I love national parks; they are big, beautiful pieces of nature that no one ever goes to.

10. Go for a walk. I go for walks all the time. As part of my health program, I wear a watch that tracks every step I take, and every day I have to hit my steps goal.

We can accomplish a great deal with a simple walk. I am walking while dictating this book, so while I am being productive and teaching you how to lower your stress, I am also lowering my own stress levels. It is a double win. To overcome our stress, we can do simple things and find pleasure in simple activities that we used to do when we are children. Sometimes we have forgotten about them because it has been too long.

11. **Go to a spa or get a massage.** These activities are specifically built around fighting stress, helping you relax, eliminating all those bad elements of your life, and helping you reset your mind.

This is a wonderful way to spend your time, and you walk out feeling reinvigorated and relaxed. You may have to go a few times to figure out exactly what you like. You may find that you like sitting in a bathtub full of mud or milk, or maybe you enjoy a massage with hot stones; just find something that works for you. Depending on where you live, this might be outside your cost range, but you do not have to go right to expensive stuff; you can be a guinea pig at the local massage school where people can learn how to massage on you. You might get a set of mixed results, but it is another way to push back against all that stress.

12. **Try pet therapy.** Studies going back to the 1980s show that we experience many health benefits when we play or interact with pets, including a reduction in our stress levels. Pets lower our blood pressure, improve our psychological well-being and self-esteem, and make us feel accepted and loved.

For those who cannot take care of a pet at home, there are pet therapy centers that offer weekly sessions with your favorite pets; the most commonly used are dogs, but you can also find rabbits, horses, guinea pigs, and even fish and crickets. Pet therapy basically provides a form of social support that can help you fight anxiety and loneliness and thus reduce your stress levels.

Even more amazing, it doesn't have to be a pet that you can touch. A recent study even found that taking care of a box of crickets can massively improve your mood.

Reflection Questions

1. If you already practice any of the techniques we discussed above, do you find them useful?
2. Which of the listed positive coping strategies do you consider most useful? If you have never tried them, what makes you think that each one will work? When and how do you plan to try them in the future?
3. Have you begun to think about these activities in new ways? Perhaps you have not thought about the things you can do to limit stress in a long time.
4. Have you spent most of your life trying to battle stress where stress is strong (in your mind) rather than outside in the real world where you have far more power? Does fighting stress in the real world seem a little bit easier? Do you feel a little more hopeful about the future?

Putting Strategies into Practice Exercise

Choose at least one (but preferably more) of the positive coping strategies we have listed in this chapter. Practice this strategy on a daily basis for the next two weeks. You should complete the questions below after the two weeks is up.

1. Do you feel stress less intensely than you did before you started using this strategy?
2. If you feel that the strategy was indeed helpful, reflect on why

you think it was helpful. If you feel that it hasn't yet been helpful, reflect on possibilities of why that might be.

3. What other positive coping strategies will you try in the future? These should include some from the list provided in this chapter, but they can also include additional ones you might have thought of or heard of.

5

WHAT IMPACT CAN STRESS HAVE ON YOUR LIFE?

There are many negative ways that stress can affect your life, and sometimes, you might not even realize that the cause of your problem is stress, or that your problem is leading to even more stress. This is how we end up in stress cycles, where something happens in our life that makes us more stressed out.

For example, say you are really worried about a project at work and cannot sleep. You are tired because you cannot sleep, so when you do try to work on your project, you cannot focus as much. Because your performance is not as good, you become more stressed out, and you enter a cycle between work, performance, and insomnia. If we understand and notice that one of the core pieces in our cycle is stress and remove that stress, we can break that cycle. It is very important to understand the different effects first.

Potential Negative Psychological and Cognitive Effects of Stress

There are many ways that stress can affect us mentally; it can affect our ability to make decisions and deal with problems. When military officers talk about battlefield strategy, they often talk about getting inside the enemy commander's decision loop. If you can affect the way your opponent is making decisions and get inside of their decision-making process, then victory is almost assured.

Stress is one of the best ways to destroy anyone's decision-making process – yours or your enemy's.

There are many ways that stress can affect our mental life, including the following:

- Problems sleeping soundly and insomnia
- Agitated and anxious behavior
- A feeling of restlessness and difficulty concentrating
- A greater tendency towards confusion
- Memory lapses
- Negative thinking
- Problems being logical
- A feeling of being overwhelmed
- Feeling irritated or frustrated
- Lacking a sense of humor
- Racing thoughts
- Frequent worry and anxiety
- Slowness in cognition
- A feeling of helplessness

Potential Negative Physical Effects of Stress

As much as stress affects the mind, it also affects the body. As I mentioned earlier, blood pressure is one indicator, but stress can also affect your health in other ways. This insidious attack on our health is similar to erosion; slowly, one drop of water at a time peels away an entire mountain. In the same way, stress can slowly eat away your health.

There are many physical manifestations of stress, including the following:

- High blood pressure

- Racing heart rate
- Heart palpitations
- Chest pain
- Cardiovascular problems
- Compromised immune system
- Hyperventilating
- Digestive problems and ulcers
- Skin rashes and acne

Potential Negative Social Effects of Stress

Stress affects our minds, it affects our bodies, and finally, it affects the way we interact with other people. Have you ever noticed that when you are feeling especially stressed out, you snap at the people in your life? Someone you care about might offer you a gentle piece of advice or some comfort, and rather than respond kindly, we snap at them. Their actions or words did not cause us to react negatively; it is our stress or emotional state.

Our emotions affect how we interpret other people's behaviors, and they can affect our ability to interact with other people. When you feel stressed out, you might withdraw from the people in your life and desire to avoid interaction. Sometimes, when I am feeling very stressed out, I want to be away from the people I love, so that my negative emotion does not affect them. In the same way, our bad mood might make our friends not want to spend time with us. Who wants to be around someone who is snapping all the time?

We might also see manifestations of this in our work life. Our stress can manifest at work and begin to cause new problems between us and our co-workers, employees, and bosses. More cracks form in our life, and stress continues to feed itself, becoming stronger and stronger.

Reflection Questions

1. Which of the psychological or cognitive effects of stress have you personally experienced? If you have not yet experienced any of the ones we've listed here, have you witnessed someone you care about suffering from any of these effects?
2. Have you experienced any of the physical effects of stress that we listed? If you have, how difficult have these problems been to deal with? How have they affected your life?
3. Have you experienced any of the social effects of stress that we listed? If you have, how have these affected your life?
4. Do you feel that stress has affected your performance in the workplace? If you feel that it has, do you feel this has had a major effect on your career? Why or why not?

6

SOCIAL PRESSURE AND STRESS

H aving people around you – family, friends, and a social community – is a critical part of what it means to be human. We are social creatures, and we yearn for human companionship. Spending time with people is often one of the best ways to push down our stress, but not always.

Sometimes, people around us can exert social pressure and peer pressure on us, and this can push us down a more stressful path. Whether they are being passive aggressive or just overloading you with extra work, sometimes, the problem and the cause of our stress is someone specific and the way they behave.

One of the ways that we exert stress on each other (sometimes intentionally, sometimes not) is by competing financially. When your friend shows off their brand-new renovated kitchen, their new car or their jet ski, you feel the pressure to try and keep up. You end up paying for a car that is out of your league or buying something you cannot afford, and it can take you years to pay it off. This is going to put extra financial pressure on you, and it all came from something quite passive in one of your friendships.

When we succumb to this kind of pressure, it negatively affects our stress levels. You are stressed by the requirement and need to fulfill this unnecessary goal. If you are unable to achieve that goal, then you feel stressed out because you cannot compete with them; you feel less. You are in a lose-lose situation, unfortunately.

Take a few moments and look at some of the sources of stress in your life. Most of us have goals that are external; they are somehow imposed by factors outside our will, and we don't even realize it. The desire to have a nicer car, or the desire to have a nicer house – a lot of that comes from other people making comments.

When I started becoming successful with my business a few years ago, the girl I was dating at the time complained about my car. She said, "Why are you driving such a cheap car if you make so much money"?

I said, "There is nothing wrong with this car; it works. It is the first car I ever bought one hundred percent on my own. It has been with me on this journey, and it means a lot to me."

I nearly ended up buying a car the cost eight times more money after that conversation. I got very close to succumbing to that level pressure, and it would have led to massive amounts of stress in my life because I left the country eight months later.

I do not even own a car now. My family owns two scooters – one we bought two years ago, and we just bought a new one this week because our first moped has fifty thousand kilometers on it. Each scooter costs ten percent of the price of the old car that my ex-girlfriend did not think was good enough.

I will most likely never own a car again. I have never purchased a brand-new car, and I think it is one the worst investments you can make. It loses most of its value the second you drive off the lot. The temptation to buy something nicer is often due to the people around us making us feel like it is something we need.

The thing about social pressure is that it plies on low self-esteem and a low level of belief in yourself. If you believe in yourself enough to not care, you do not need to compete. If our strengths and our goals come from within instead of outside, then we can eliminate one of the sources of stress in our life.

We can get caught up in a cycle where we think, "I have to have the best [this or that] because if I don't have the coolest stuff, people won't like me; I won't fit in, and people will look down on me." We do not want to be the "poor friend." We do not want to be the one friend who does not have a car and always has to ask for a ride.

But the people who actually care about you like you for *you*, not for your stuff. It is not a competition. Their friendship is not about material items you have or the way you spend your money. Honestly, if you have friends that are all about the money and objects, you need to excise them from your life.

Occasionally, throughout my life, I have eliminated friendships because I realized they were toxic, and they were affecting my emotions and my health negatively. If people are not genuine about their friendship with you, then why do you care what they think of you anyway?

Here is a simple question to ask yourself: does it make sense to put financial stress on yourself just to impress someone who is only friends with you because of those things? They are only friends with your possessions, not you. It does not make sense, does it? In fact, it is absurd.

Below is a test that will give you a good idea whether or not social pressure is affecting you in negative ways.

Social Pressure Test

Stress can affect your friendships and relationships; it can affect how we interpret people's behavior and how we react to the world around us. We can measure our level of stress and how much it is affecting our lives by taking this simple test. Please take the time to think about these questions and answer each question as openly and honestly as you can.

1. You just had someone come over to your house for dinner. This person made a disparaging remark about your dining room table. What are you thinking?

a) I need to get a new dining room table as soon as possible! This one must look horrible if this person thought they should make a remark.

b) That person was extremely rude, and I will think twice before inviting them over again.

2. It seems like all of your friends are always going out to lunch at expensive bistros. You have started going into debt in your desperation to fit in. What do you do?

a) You continue to go into debt, just to fit in.

b) You calmly explain to your friends that your budget doesn't allow you to go to all of their lunches, but that maybe they can come over to your house instead sometimes. If you get a negative or snobbish reaction, you simply think that person or those people weren't really your friends in the first place!

3. It seems like everyone you know has a membership at a health club. You find health club membership fees too hefty for your current budget, and you find it easy to stay in shape using simpler methods. What do you do?

a) I want to fit in, so I join a health club.

b) Is there something to do? I just carry on with what I'm doing!

4. Many people in your neighborhood have recently installed pools in their backyards. You feel a bit left out, but a pool is simply not in your budget for any time in the foreseeable future. What do you do?

a) I look into ways I could get a pool, even if it means I will have to go into debt.

b) Nothing! What would I do?

5. Certain people you know are always talking about "galas" and

other formal events they seemingly attend on a regular basis. You feel awkward, as you never really attend such events because they tend to be very expensive. You feel left out of conversations because of this. What do you do?

a) I try to find some galas or other formal events to go to and spend some money on formal dresses or suits.

b) I go to dinner and a movie instead!

6. You are attending a pub quiz with some new friends, and a hard question comes up. You know the answer, but when you tell the group, they say they're not sure and don't write down what you suggested. What do you do?

a) I shut up and let them decide what to write. I want them to like me and accept me in the group, not to think I am arrogant!

b) I repeat that I know the answer, and I explain why I am absolutely sure it is correct.

7. You have been queuing at the post office for over twenty minutes, and when it's finally your turn, someone jumps the queue and goes straight to the counter. What do you do?

a) Nothing; they probably had an emergency or something very urgent to do.

b) I tap on their shoulder and gently point out that I was next in the queue.

SCORING: THE MORE "A" answers you chose, the more susceptible you tend to be to social pressure. If you chose a lot of "a" answers, you need to do some work on improving your senses of self-confidence and self-esteem. Your opinion about yourself and your feelings about yourself should not be dependent on what other people think.

Exercise Five

After looking at your results from the previous test, you may have noticed that stress is affecting your social life in ways you have never been aware of before. It is a new problem you are suddenly discovering, and the danger of stress affecting your social life and relationships is that it can become stronger.

As we pull away from people or people pull away from us, we become more isolated, stress can become more powerful, and other negative emotions can slip through the cracks, like depression, anxiety, and anger. We want to nip those in the bud. For this exercise:

1. Create a list of the ways you are going to combat the effects of stress on your social life. What are some actions you can start taking now to improve your social interactions?

2. A week from now, after you have written down your plans in your Conquer Stress Journal, reflect on their impact.

a. Does your social life feel better?

b. Do you feel a little bit more connected to the people around you?

c. Have the people around you noticed your behavior altering?

d. Has anyone made a comment?

e. If you feel like your efforts have not made much of a difference, what can you do to improve that?

f. Do you need to try harder or do you need more focus?

g. Did a new cause of stress enter your life?

We want to become people who are reflective; we want to be aware of our emotions and how they are affecting our lives, so we can then change them. This is how we can become more powerful. I would like you to think about ways you can improve the list you have been working on for the last week and improve and build upon this progress, so you can become even more successful in removing the negative effects of stress in your social life.

7

REDUCING THE STRESS LEVEL OF YOUR LIFESTYLE

There are many different angles from which we can approach stress. We have talked about fighting stress in the real world, we covered activities that distract you and remove stress in your life, and we mentioned how exercise, hobbies, and many other activities can be helpful.

Sometimes though, we can be in a situation where none of those apply. I know that you cannot leave to go hit the batting cages for two hours every time you are working on a project at work. Sometimes you have to work your way through a project and stick with a stressful task.

In this chapter, we are going to focus on tactics and strategies that you can use when you are dealing with something stressful, and how you can decrease your level of stress when something seems to be overwhelming.

Stress-Reduction Strategies

There are many things that we can do to deal with stress effectively in our day-to-day operations.

1. **Be more organized.** Stress is often the result of disorganization and things taking longer than they should or us spending too long looking for a piece of information. Whenever I cannot find a file and have to search for it, it slows down the rest of the process, and that search starts to feel like a wasted effort, which plants the seeds of more stress and chaos.

Sometimes it feels counterproductive. We tell ourselves that we are already behind on the project, and there is no time to get organized. That is something we say to ourselves, but the problem just gets bigger, and we could have dealt with it at the beginning in just a few hours.

There is an old Latin aphorism I learned in high school, "Mens sana in corpore sano," which means a sound mind in a sound body. This applies to the world around you. When trying to pack a suitcase, if all your clothes are crumpled up, they will not fit in right, but if everything is folded, everything will fit in easily. It is exactly the same for organization; when things are organized, more things can fit in your life, less space is wasted, and inefficiency disappears.

Every time I improve organization in my life, the quality of my work and my efficiency also improve, and my stress levels lower accordingly. It is worth taking a day to reorganize the areas of your life that need it the most. If you are disorganized in the house or with your children, or if the children's toys are all over the place, maybe you need another cabinet, or maybe you just need to work on where everything should be stored. If your computer is cluttered, spend some time working your way through a decluttering strategy.

Being able to find all those pieces of information more quickly will reveal more time that you thought was lost. Some people spend up to six hours a day checking emails at work; in an eight-hour workday, seventy-five percent of their time is spent going through emails and communicating ineffectively.

2. **Be open to delegating.** For a long time, this was a struggle for me. The first time I tried to grow my company several years ago, I hired a

bunch of staff who were very inefficient, and I ended up working for them rather than them working for me. I started to notice that if I took my eyes off my employees, they would work less and demand pay raises.

It was a very stressful experience. I learned from my mistakes, and I learned that the problem is not hiring people and building a team; the problem was in my organization and in how I delegated. I now have a growing team, but it has increased my effectiveness and lowered my stress because I know I can finish things much faster. I know what each member of my team is capable of, I know their assignments each week, and we have a very good organizational structure.

Delegating and passing on tasks is very hard at first, and it is tempting to micromanage; you want to watch every little step of the process, and that usually comes from perfectionism or not trusting your team, but whatever the cause, it limits your effectiveness. If you are only able to do what you can do by yourself each week, then your maximum effectiveness is limited by your time. If you are able to delegate to other people, each person you can pass on to magnifies your influence. If you have ten employees, you can accomplish ten times more in a week. And the best part is you do not have to handle everything yourself; it is too overwhelming.

3. Be merciful with yourself. We often hold ourselves to a higher standard than we do to anyone else around us. It is very tempting to hold myself to a higher standard than I do my family, my co-workers, and my employees.

Sometimes, it is tempting to do someone else's job just so that it gets done, and your eight-hour day turns into ten or twelve hours. Whether you are carrying stress for tasks that you delegated and completed quickly or from your own tasks because you keep asking yourself to do more than you're physically capable of doing, all these things can become too much.

It is good to be disciplined and organized, but you also have to be honest with yourself about what you can bear and how much work you can accomplish. Sometimes, we say we can do a job that we cannot actually do. I do the same thing; sometimes, I want to do everything that people bring to me. It is tempting to take on all these extra projects, and then you cannot handle them physically or time-wise, and you end up having to work a massive amount of overtime simply because you overpromise.

This can come from a desire to do as many projects as possible, or a need to please everyone. You are constantly looking for affirmation externally. Whatever the cause is, be fastidious and diligent about the promises you make and the tasks you take on. Make sure that they are tasks you can handle and complete in the time you have available.

4. Allow yourself leisure and fun. You have to build breaks in your schedule. Whenever I start new projects, I start working too much and putting in so many hours that other areas of my life start to suffer. Working fourteen-hour days because you are excited hurts you just as much as working those fourteen-hour days because you are behind schedule.

Leisure activities de-stress you; they maintain your health and your balance. Just like you cannot keep working without eating and sleeping, you cannot keep working without bringing in some de-stressing activities; your body is meant to work on a cycle, and you have to maintain that balance.

5. Control how you measure success. We live in a society where most definitions of success are external; everyone tells us how we should measure our levels of success. Two to three times a week, someone will say something to me about owning a house. I am just not a big fan of owning a house. I have no desire to own one.

There used to be this concept that owning a house would give you a sense of security, but if you have been alive as long as I have, you have seen many people lose their houses. People spend years trying to pay off a mortgage, but when something happens, and they cannot make a payment for a few months, they lose the house that they thought they owned. You do not really own a house if you have a mortgage; you are renting it from the bank with terrible terms.

Once you have paid off your house, you still have to pay certain taxes and insurance every single year, and the government decides what your house is worth. How many times have you seen people spend their lives paying off their house, taking care of it, being fastidious with it, and looking forward to the day when they can pass it on to their children? Then, when they pass away, the children cannot afford the taxes to keep the house, so they sell it.

Real estate agents, banks, and the taxman can say whatever they want, but until someone gives you the money for something, it is not worth anything. Yet we think the measurement of success is how much money we make, how many houses we own or how nice our house or car is. We end up in these cycles where we are using old measurements of success.

Take a moment to reset and think what is more important. Then dig deeper, and each time you answer a question, ask yourself "why." What is the most important thing to you?

"I want to make a bunch of money" Why?

"I want to buy cool stuff." Why?

Is it because you want to show it to other people? Well, then you have a problem. You are in the system because you are not controlling your happiness. You will only be happy when other people like your stuff.

I measure success in how much time I spend doing things I like, impacting other people's lives, and spending time with my family. I take my children swimming three or four times a day. To me, that is worth far more than a bigger house. We do not have a very big house, but it is big enough for what we need. We could move somewhere more expensive, but it would be financially stressful for me to afford. I could do that if I worked extra hours, but I would have to spend less time around the children. I'm not willing to make that trade – I know that my children will remember the time they spent with their father far more than the size of our house.

Take some time to think about what matters to you; focus on values, goals, dreams, and missions that come from within you, not externally. Just because everyone else says you should have a specific goal or earn a specific amount of money does not mean it is going to work for you because often, we hit those goals, and it does not make us happy anyway. That is a great lie of our culture; we spend ages chasing a goal, and then we get there and go, "Well, this is not great."

6. Avoid procrastination. Putting things off is the absolute worst. There is nothing worse than realizing you are behind schedule. I am dealing with this at the moment, even though technically I did not procrastinate; I was working on other projects because I thought it was ahead of my transcriptionist, but it is the same feeling. I have to record even if I do not feel like it because if I don't, she doesn't have any work.

I have an entire book about procrastination because it is such a big problem it can be devastating. Waiting to the last minute to work on a project or being behind schedule is incredibly stressful, and time pressure affects the quality of your work.

7. Learn to accept what you cannot change. If there are things in your life that stress you out and you cannot affect them, just accept them. I have seen people say on Twitter that their politician did not win an election, therefore now they cannot do their job, or they have to see a psychologist five times a week.

Those are things outside of our control; I cannot change who the president is. Why worry about the things that you cannot affect? If reading the newspaper stresses you out, stop reading it.

I am continually lowering the amount of time I invest in the news every day. These days, I spend five minutes a day reading the headlines to see if anything is relevant to me, and then I move on (and I still do not feel good). I never feel good about what I read in the news.

Stop worrying about the things you cannot affect or change. Focus on just your life and doing the best you can, and you will find that a great deal of stress just fades away. Worrying about things you cannot affect is one of the greatest wastes of time possible.

8. Watch out for everything you can to avoid unnecessary stress. There are loads of ways that we can waste energy by bringing stress into our lives with no benefits whatsoever.

Common Sources of Unnecessary Stress

1. Giving in to social pressure is often a source of unnecessary stress, especially when it has to do with superficial and status-oriented issues. Very rarely does succumbing to social pressure or peer pressure lead to something good. Think about every after-school special you watched when you were younger. Have you ever seen a scenario where someone gets peer-pressured into doing something, and it ends well? Like the time someone got talked into taking steroids, study medication, or illegal drugs or drinking when they were fifteen years old. Every single time it ends poorly, and yet we can succumb to peer pressure as adults because we think it is not the same thing.

2. Taking on more responsibilities than necessary at home or at work. Sometimes, when we have very unbalanced relationships, or when we take on jobs other people should be doing, it can be too much for one person to bear. Some people look at my relationship from the outside and judge it because they do not understand.

My wife does not work, and she will. There are a host of reasons for that, and I went into my relationship with the expectation that she would never work once we started dating. My wife comes from a Third World country and has a limited education; even if she got the best job she possibly could, she would make less in a month than I do in a single day. That is the first of many reasons why I work and she does not.

However, this does not mean that there is no balance in our relationship. My wife runs the whole house – she manages the house budget, she takes care of the children, she makes schooling decisions and takes care of our food. All of that eliminates a massive amount of stress from my life.

All these little things add up, and if I had to think about all these tasks from other areas of life, my work would suffer.

We have a partnership, and while I carry one hundred percent of the work burdens and provide the finances for our family, she handles close to one hundred percent of the home-related responsibilities. This is a division of power that works best in our relationship. My sister and her husband are both lawyers, and they have a different division of labor within their family.

Everything is different in each relationship, and you want to find the best balance of responsibilities that works for you based on your strengths and the number of things that you can handle. When I was single, I did things very differently. I handled my food very differently, and I was responsible for cleaning my house, organization, and rent.

One of the best things of being in a relationship is that you can find a great balance for what each of you does based on what you are great at, and this removes some of the stress from your life. In every area of your life, do not take on too much responsibility. You can say, "No, I cannot do that; it is too much, and I will not be able to do a good job." It is hard, but learning to say no will help you to reduce your stress levels.

3. Focus on things you cannot control. This is where we get caught worrying about the future and thinking about "what if" scenarios. If you get caught up in these cycles, you can end up spending your entire life living for an event that might never happen.

How many people were waiting for Y2K (the Millennium bug) or the world to end the year 2000 and then nothing happened? All that stress and effort was wasted. This does not mean you should not be prepared, and it's certainly fine to have food in your basement and a plan to make sure your family can survive for six months if something does happen, but it should not be what you think about all the time. It should not be something that stresses you out all the time.

4. Getting trapped in negative thought cycles is a core source of unnecessary stress. Be aware of your thought life; notice when a negative thought infects your mind and actively push it away. Say, "No thanks, sorry thought I do not need you. That is ridiculous. I am not going to worry about that one."

Stray thoughts can be poisonous, but we have the ability and the power to reject them. That is why we talked about meditation earlier - to strengthen your ability to push away unnecessary negative thoughts.

Reflection Questions

1. Brainstorm a list of sources of unnecessary stress in your life. Make sure to give yourself a substantial amount of time to think about this. You will probably be surprised by how many sources you come up with.
2. In your Conquer Stress Journal, discuss how you will use two or more of the stress-reduction strategies listed in the first part of this chapter. Describe how you will incorporate them into your daily life.
3. Make a plan for a leisurely, relaxing morning, afternoon, or entire day. Decide how and when you will carry out your plan.
4. Do you tend to procrastinate? If you do, how do you feel this habit has affected your stress level? Reflect on things you could do to make you less likely to procrastinate.

5. What changes to your lifestyle do you think could reduce your general level of stress? Are you willing to make these changes? Why or why not? If you want to make these changes, how will you go about doing so?

6. Do you tend to think in a negative way? If so, do you find that you are sometimes or often too critical of yourself?

7. Do you feel that you need to delegate more responsibilities and duties? If so, how could you go about doing this?

8. How do you tend to think about success? Now that you've had a chance to reflect on this, do you feel that you should broaden your definition of success? If your answer is yes, brainstorm things that you think you should bring into your concept of success. Reflect on how incorporating these things into your definition of success would help reduce the pressure and stress you experience in your life.

9. How could you better organize your work environment and your life in general? How do you feel that improving your organization could help reduce your stress level?

10. How good are you at having a feeling of acceptance regarding things you can't change? How do you think you could improve in this regard? How do you feel that improving in this area could reduce your stress levels?

8

STRESS AND HEALTH

W e know that stress has major health implications and can affect you in many different ways. It can cause new diseases or accelerate existing ones, magnifying your health problems significantly.

Here are ten of the most common problems connected to stress. You might not even be aware of all of them:

1. Obesity
2. Disorders of the gastrointestinal system
3. Headaches
4. Anxiety and depression
5. Heart disease
6. Respiratory problems, such as asthma
7. Diabetes
8. Acceleration of aging
9. Alzheimer's disease
10. High blood pressure

Meditation

We already know that there is a powerful interrelationship between stress and health, between the mind and the body. We can have a mental cause of stress that leads to health problems in our bodies, and enough stress can end your life early.

We can fight stress either in the mind or in the body, and activities that combine the mind and the body can be very effective. One of the most powerful ones is the practice of meditation. Many people scoff when they first hear about meditation or think that it is ridiculous. We often think of it as a religious practice, and if we are not religious or not particular Eastern religions, we think that meditation is not for us.

We also say things like, "I do not have time." We imagine that meditation takes an hour every single day and is a huge hassle, so any benefits we might experience from relaxing our minds and our bodies will be more than subsumed by the stress of the time we have lost.

We get caught in this pincer where we think that trying to meditate will take a lot of time and will cause more problems, but five to twenty minutes a day are more than enough to relax and diffuse yourself.

We are going to cover several types of meditation that you can experiment with to help you start to reduce those painful stress levels.

1. **Focus-based or concentration-based meditation.** This is where you simply focus on one thing and try to push away all other thoughts. You can do this by looking at a spot on the wall, a candle, or a picture. You can even use one of those pictures that were very popular when I was in high school, where you have to cross your eyes to try and see the boat hidden in the image.

Perhaps you prefer sound or a smell; you can experiment with different things. Some people think of a bell noise when they think of meditation, and that can work; the bell makes a distinctive sound, and if we focus on that sound, it is very relaxing and soothing. The goal of this type of meditation is to push away all the extraneous thoughts.

We are always thinking about six or seven things at a time, and this is a way that we can empty all of those wasted buckets occupied by stressful and unnecessary things and cleanse your mental palate.

2. Mindfulness meditation. What is beautiful about mindfulness meditation is that you can do it anytime, anywhere. You simply decide to live in the moment, and you focus totally on what you are doing, ignoring the past in the future.

This is what I experience when I am in the ocean. It is very hard for me to surf and think about what I need to do tomorrow at the same time. You absolutely can do other things while practicing mindfulness meditation; the idea is to simply get totally engaged with your body and think about what you are doing to the point where you push everything else way.

When I was sixteen, this is how I drove. Driving took so much of my attention and focus that there was nothing else I could do or think of. With time, we get to the point where we can drive without thinking about it. We become so good at certain things that we have to move on from them.

3. Movement meditation. This is where we do something physical that has a meditation component to it, such as walking meditation or yoga. We often think of trendy Western yoga (like hot yoga, hard rock yoga or adding in crazy music), but traditional yoga is based on very slow movements.

You can also enjoy Tai Chi, an ancient Chinese martial art that is all about very slow movements. Moving slowly is harder than moving fast; if you try tai chi for just one hour, you will see it is really hard. We make this false assumption that moving slowly is easier than moving fast, but it is often the opposite. Moving slowly requires precision and extreme focus, which is the aim of meditation.

4. Body scan meditation. With this type of meditation, you scan your body like a CAT Scan or laser either from the top to the bottom or from the bottom to the top, and you become aware of each and every part of your body. You focus on the bottoms of your feet, then your toes and tops of your feet, then your ankles, and you slowly work your way up and become aware of every sensation within your body.

When was the last time you thought about how the ground feels?

When was the last time you thought about how your back feels and how the clothes feel on your body?

We have so many sensations at any given time that we train our brains to block out extraneous or repetitive information.

When you go into a room that smells bad, after a few minutes you cannot smell it anymore; your body still knows it is there, but your brain is deleting that information because it knows you already have it. You know what your clothes feel like, so you do not pay attention to them anymore. But you can reactivate those nerves in your body and focus on how your muscles feel. How does it feel when you swallow in your throat? How does each breath feel as it enters and leaves your body?

With any type of meditation, and especially when combined with exercise, you want to try and slow down your breathing. Slowing down and being in the moment is what allows you to relax your body and your brain and to push down those stress levels.

You do not need to sit in a traditional lotus posture with your hands face up on each of your knees in order to meditate. You can choose any position you want, whether sitting in a chair or on a mat. Here we just want to realize that practice can be very useful, and then you can find your own type of meditation.

The Effect of Exercise

Exercising your body is very beneficial. For most of us, stress manifests very strongly mentally, which is why, as with all mental diseases, challenges, or obstacles, I recommend fighting it in your body. Exercising releases all sorts of endorphins and chemicals in your body that kill and remove stress. This is why we see people who are very stressed out become amazing athletes; they go on long bike rides, they go boxing, they go for a run – anything that pushes away their stress and makes them feel better. This is why people become addicted to exercise - because it feels good.

Finding a sport or an exercise that you like will make a big difference. When you think of exercise, you do not have to think of going to the gym with an annoying personal trainer and everyone looking at you like you have the worst body in the room. You can do something that you enjoy, even if it is something simple.

Start playing dodgeball or softball or kickball; there are adult sports leagues in every town. It is a great way to both be around other people and do a fun sport. Exercise does not have to be horrible; we want to do things that are fun, which means we are more likely to go back and do it regularly.

Exercise Six

For five days in a row this week, try a new physical activity; it can be aerobics, Zumba, yoga, baseball, the batting cages – anything that you do where you exercise and get your heart pumping for thirty minutes to an hour. At the end of the week, answer the following questions in your Journal:

1. How do you feel your stress level is right now? Do you feel that your stress level is lowering? Do you feel that your exercise regime, with the sport you are playing, is benefiting you?

2. How do you feel that this new physical regime is affecting your overall health?

3. If you are struggling with some of the health problems we talked about earlier in this book, are any of them gone away or diminished?

4. Are you surprised by the positive impact that exercise is having in your life?

5. Are you going to commit and continue this exercise regime or are you going to quit after these five days and go back to your old ways?

6. What is your plan for implementing and adding exercise into your life in the long term? How will you implement this practice from here on out?

9

SHORT CASE STUDIES

I n this chapter, we are going to examine some fictional case studies. Sometimes it can be hard to look at ourselves objectively. It helps to take the role of the observer looking from the outside, as we search for tactics and strategies for dealing with our stress. After each study, you are going to answer some multiple-choice and reflection questions to help you improve your insight and bring you a little bit closer to victory over stress in your life.

CASE STUDY 1. One of Edith's family members is sick. Trying to care for a loved one while dealing with her own medical problems is becoming overwhelming. The doctor has told Edith that stress is making her health problems worse.

Write a paragraph giving Edith some advice on how she can reduce the effect of stress on her physical health.

CASE STUDY 2. Meredith has the lowest income of all of her friends and family, and she often feels left out of activities and conversations. Her friends and family aren't doing anything to try to make her feel included. In fact, some of them even make snide comments about her lack of money.

Write a paragraph giving Meredith some advice on how she can reduce the impact of her lesser income on her emotional health.

CASE STUDY 3. Jack has developed negative habits for dealing with his stress, including smoking, drinking to excess, and general risk-taking. These problems are starting to affecting his relationships both at home and at work. They are even beginning to affect his health.

Write a paragraph giving Jack some advice on how he can stop relying on negative coping habits and develop some positive coping methods to replace them. How can you convince him of the importance of changing his habits?

CASE STUDY 4. Mary is skeptical about the benefits of meditation and doesn't think she'll be able to learn how to relax. Her stress is already affecting her health – she often experiences a racing heartbeat, and sometimes she has trouble catching her breath.

Write a paragraph giving Mary some advice on how meditation could help her cope with her stress. How can meditation reduce the effects of stress on her body?

CASE STUDY 5. Jane is feeling very stressed at work. Her manager is constantly increasing her workload without increasing her pay or thanking her for all her extra effort. Jane is developing a severe case of anxiety that she feels is an unavoidable consequence of keeping her job.

Write a paragraph giving Jane some advice on how she could cope with the situation to reduce the stress that is causing her anxiety. Is there a way she can manage how much work she accepts from her overzealous manager?

CASE STUDY **6.** Max's friends own so many nice things that he keeps increasing his debt trying to keep up with them. Vacations, concerts, and cars are all weighing down his shoulders. His friends don't even realize how hard it is for him to keep up with their expensive lifestyles, so he feels like he can't talk to them about the pressure he's under.

How would you advise Max to approach his financial situation and relationships? Where should he focus his first de-stressing efforts? How can he begin to deal with this growing issue?

10

BUILDING YOUR SELF-CONFIDENCE

You may be wondering why there is a whole chapter on self-confidence in a book on stress. They might seem like two pretty different problems, but if you go back a few chapters and think about social pressure, you will see how we can sometimes get drawn into making poor decisions that put additional stress on us when we succumb to this pressure.

It is time to strengthen your compass, so it is easier for you to make the decisions that you know you should make anyway, and you do not feel bad when you make bad decisions because you can avoid them now.

Self-confidence gives you a greater sense of your ability to accomplish things and to deal with the complexities of life. The stronger you get with your confidence, and the more competent you feel, the less stressed you are because you know you can handle surprising situations and you are ready for them.

This begs the ultimate question: how can you build up your self-confidence?

Ways to Boost Your Self Confidence

I am going to share with you ten different techniques to build up your self-confidence. If you implement these techniques, you will notice massive changes in your life.

1. **Work on your self-image.** Your self-image is the picture you see of yourself in your mind. Often, there is a big difference between what we see in the mirror and what we see in our minds. Very rarely are people accurate in how they perceive themselves, but we want to try and push ourselves more towards accuracy. It is better to have an image that is too good than one that is too bad. Take the time to assess yourself and your perception of yourself. Is the way you see yourself determined or affected by things other people have said?

When I am working one-on-one with someone through a coaching process, I often discover that they have run into the same hurdle for years or decades, and it all came from a comment that someone made when they were very young.

There are a lot of books, stories, and psychological techniques for dealing with this problem, which is often called a "wound" because it is an injury that happened a long time ago but has not healed. Someone can plant a hurtful word in your mind that becomes a highlight reel that passes through your mind all the time. You start to think you are not good enough to do certain things.

If we look for confidence from things outside of us, our image or sense of self will always be fractured and flawed because what we see is a distorted image. It is like when you are in one of those elevators that have a mirror on both sides, and there are thousands of reflections. You go further and further away, but each reflection is a little more flawed. We want to get back to normal; if you have negative memories from your past that you think about all the time, it is worth going through a process to eliminate them.

2. Avoid procrastination. The first book in the *Habit of Success* series is about procrastination for a reason; it is the root cause of many problems. Just today, I received an email from someone asking how I am so productive and get so many things done. I fight against procrastination all the time.

Many people talk about how they operate better under pressure and brag about things that are actually unpleasant and counterproductive,

"I can operate on four hours of sleep a night,"

"I work sixteen-hour days,"

"I work better under pressure,"

"I am so much better when there is a deadline, and I am late."

Everyone I know who bragged about those things to me ten and twenty years ago has suffered in a different, dramatic way. Some of them are no longer in the same careers because they cracked, and it's not surprising.

Procrastination manifests itself in different ways, and people have found ways to justify it and make it sound great that you can operate well under pressure, but you should not have to be there. You should not require pressure to get the job done. I always try to finish projects early. In fact, I recently shifted how I estimate projects by adding fifty percent to the time so that there is no risk of me being late.

I am learning to better manage expectations and give myself a little more breathing room. I do not need pressure; it is better to promise ninety days and deliver in sixty. That is the real power of conquering procrastination – under-promise and over-deliver.

3. Break a sweat. One of the great benefits of the problem with my eyes is that I have to work outside. I dictate these books because I cannot write on a computer anymore, due to my vision problems. I work on a little dock, pacing up and down as I dictate. My watch tracks every step I take, and I am sweating while writing this chapter.

Exercise releases endorphins into your bloodstream and helps your body run more smoothly. Your body is a machine designed to be used, and there are many different ways we can add exercise into our life.

It is very possible that the last thing you want to do is go to the gym every day; the thought of trying to keep up with the regulars and spending all of that money to look at those bodies is certainly not enticing; you don't want to feel like you are the worst person in the gym.

There are plenty of ways to get great exercise without setting foot in a gym. Look up adult sports leagues in your area. Join a Frisbee team. Guess what – throwing Frisbee is fun and not stressful. There are loads of sports you can go outside, play in the park and sweat a little bit but with no pressure. There is none of the uncomfortableness of going to the gym. The cost is much lower, and it's more fun; it's a double win.

Sports are way better than just going to the gym because you also have a smile on your face, so you hit the stress on two different levels. Your self-esteem is going to go up, and you will feel more confident in yourself and more comfortable with who you are.

4. Set small goals and keep track of your achievements. Most of us cannot remember what we achieved in the past. When it comes to confidence, it is almost like, "What have you done for me lately?" But if you sit down and make a list of all of the different things you have accomplished in your life and all of your successes, you could probably come up with a list of hundreds of things you have not thought about in years.

The last time I made one of these lists, I was surprised at all the different things I remembered – things I had not thought about in decades.

You have done things that matter and things you are proud of; it is worth memorializing and remembering them. You can start now with a little journal or task-tracker – something that keeps a record of your accomplishments.

Tracking your goals and progress is extremely valuable. This is why I continually encourage you to fill out and track yourself in your Conquer Stress Journal.

5. Change your posture. Psychology and physiology are deeply inter-twined; if you smile for five minutes, you will feel happy. The way you hold your body affects your confidence.

There is a reason why soldiers act differently than everyone else. One of the first things soldiers learn is how to stand at attention. I wish I had better posture, but when I actively walk and hold my posture up using the correct technique, I feel different. Imagine that there is a string going through the top your head all the way down to your feet, holding you up like a puppet.

With good posture, you will feel stronger and more confident. Try this technique, and you will notice a difference immediately. When you are slouched, people treat you differently, and you act differently. A little change in posture goes a long way.

6. Speak slow. The slower and more confidently you speak, the more people will listen to you. I will be honest with you; this is something that I struggle with. I tend to speak very quickly, espe-cially when I am excited because I spent years training myself to speak quickly. I was on the debate team in high school, and a big component of high school policy debate is saying as many things you can inside a time limit. You have eight minutes to make as many arguments as possible, and the team who can speak faster often wins.

What was the gift of the time has turned into a curse for the rest of my life. Sometimes people misinterpret the speed at which I talk as a sign of low self-confidence. I have to intentionally slow down when I talk.

This also applies to the way you walk. I am a slow walker. I always have been and always will be. If you are going to hike with me, you will hate me. Even my wife always ends up three steps ahead of me, no matter where we are walking; it does not matter that I am taller and have longer legs.

For a long time, people would pressure me to walk faster, and I felt this need to conform. When I changed the way I thought about it, everything around me changed. I started telling people that I walk slow and they should wait for me; I am important. I even created a name for it; I called it "high-value walking."

The president can walk as slow as he wants, and everyone else will slow down. It is the mailroom guy who has to run fast and keep up with the boss. Walking and talking slowly will improve your confidence. When you know what you are doing is intentional, you are demonstrating to your body and the world around you a great belief in yourself.

7. Be prepared for your tasks. The more you prepare in advance, the better. When we procrastinate, we end up in situations that we're not ready for. How many times have you been or you have known the guy who has to go clean his car before a date?

When you switch and become someone whose car is always clean and ready, you do not have that kind of stress, and you can spend time focusing on other positive elements before your dates.

This applies to many other areas of life. I am about to start writing my first fiction book, and I would love to be out there dictating it right now. I have already written two outlines, but it is not yet ready. Even though I am excited to see how I can do in the world of fiction, the preparation is not ready. I know that if I started to dictate the introduction or one of the chapters, I would stumble because I have not made all of the decisions; I have not prepared everything. I need a deeper and layered outline. Preparing makes life easier.

8. Challenge negative thinking. This is getting a little bit metacognitive because we are thinking about thinking. When you have a negative thought, I want you to isolate it. Look at that negative thought and go, "Where did this come from? Why am I having this thought? Is this based on reality?"

Sometimes you have a negative thought, and you think, "I wish I had done something." It happens, but just remind yourself, "There is no value in worrying about the past. I do not have a time machine, therefore dwelling on the past is a waste because I cannot affect it." This is mindfulness; this is being in the moment, and it is an important part of confidence.

We don't want to waste time and energy thinking and worrying about things that have no value. Every time a negative thought comes in your life, ask yourself why you're thinking it.

At first, you may only be able to become aware of the negative thoughts. That is the first step in the process; you are identifying the enemy. As you get better at identifying it and understanding the cause of these bad thoughts, you will become better and better at banishing and defeating them as well.

9. Replace negative thoughts with positive thinking. Actively encourage yourself and train yourself to think positively. People often say "think positive" or "feel better about yourself" or "work on your self-esteem." But how do you actually implement that?

Allow me to share with you how I do it. When I want to improve my confidence and my positive thinking, I compliment myself inside my head. You may even do it outside or in front of a mirror. Every time I have a negative thought, I say, "I just thought I am fat; I need to think two positive thoughts to make up for it." That can be your simple process; every time you have a negative thought, you go, "Okay, I have to think of two positive things to counterbalance." Eventually, this will go from an active to a passive process, and you will begin to think positively without even trying.

10. Be a lifelong learner. The moment you stop learning new things, your brain begins to atrophy. Your brain can only be in one of two states: learning or forgetting. There is no middle area where your brain is caught in stasis, magically frozen in time. It's either one or the other.

As you develop more skills and techniques and learn how to do new things, you improve your sense of self-efficacy. That is your belief in your ability to accomplish and do things – your competence. You increase the size of your wheelhouse, the area of your expertise, and the way you feel about yourself will be better.

The more you know how to deal with problems, and the more you know how to overcome challenges, the better. That comes from trying new things, whether it is learning a new language or learning how to start a fire without using a lighter.

Reflection Questions

1. Before reading this chapter, did you realize how much of an effect self-confidence can have on your ability to deal with stress?
2. Honestly appraise your current sense of self-confidence. How weak or strong is your self-confidence at this moment?
3. Now that you have read our tips for improving your self-confidence, which of them do you think you'll try first? Why will you choose them? Or do you think you will try all of them? That's definitely a good idea!
4. How do you feel that your current sense of self-confidence has either helped or hindered your ability to deal with stress with the least impact on yourself possible?

Exercise Seven: Before and After

1. Practice at least five of the listed techniques for improving self-confidence for at least one week. After that, answer the following

questions in your Conquer Stress Journal:

a) Do you feel that your sense of self-confidence has improved? Why or why not? If it has improved, in what ways do you feel it has gotten better?

b) Do you think that your self-confidence would have improved even more if you had made use of more of the techniques? Are there techniques you haven't put to use yet that you feel might be especially useful to you? Why do you think this is the case?

2. What have you learned about yourself by putting these techniques into practice? Are you surprised about your level of self-confidence? Was it weaker or stronger than you had originally thought?

3. If your self-confidence has improved, how do you feel that your stronger sense of self-confidence has positively impacted your life? How do you feel it has strengthened your ability to deal with stress with less impact on your mental and physical health?

Exercise Eight: Self-Image

In your Conquer Stress Journal, describe yourself on the left-hand side of the page. Be totally honest. If there are negative pieces to your self-image, if you think you are ugly or you do not like your teeth or you think that your hair is the wrong color – any of those little thoughts, write them down. We need to be very honest here; it is going to be a little bit painful when you have to write down those negative things, but it is absolutely critical.

No one else is going to see this; you do not have to show it to anybody. Then, on the right-hand side of the page, write down your ideal self-image – describe your 2.0 version. Write down how you would like to see yourself in six months and what you want to change about your self-image.

Imagine that you are this person and pretend you are the 2.0 version of yourself all the time. Eventually, if you keep acting like this person, you will become the 2.0 version of yourself.

Exercise Nine: Avoiding Procrastination

Look at something in your life that you like to avoid or wait to do until the last-minute, whether this is exercise, spending time with your family, calling your in-laws, or working on specific projects. Find something in your life where you want to procrastinate and then make a commitment in your Conquer Stress Journal to fight against this temptation to procrastinate.

Track your progress in the Journal, and write down every time you have a thought about taking a little time off. You may find that simply writing it down makes you more likely to do the job because you don't want to have to write down that you slacked off; it feels bad. No one wants to turn themselves in, but the Fifth Amendment won't protect you here. This little technique will make a difference for you, and maybe for a while, this is what you need to do.

If your procrastination problem is really big, then I definitely recommend reading my book on the subject, because I go into great detail on how to directly face and conquer this ugly beast. For right now, try this tactic and see how effective it is for you.

Exercise Ten: Walking

Walking is so good for you! It is one of the best ways to improve your health and keep your body working and in good condition. I wear a watch the tracks every step I take, and I do recommend getting something to help you develop a walking habit.

There are many ways to strengthen this habit. Start listening to audiobooks, with the rule that you can only listen while walking. When you are locked into a really engaging story, the desire to hear the next chapter will have you chomping at the bit to lace up your walking sneakers.

I am not asking you to run; just go for a walk around the neighborhood, clearing your head. Listen to your favorite music or a podcast. Find a way to make walking enjoyable, and you will be more likely to stick with it.

11

WHAT HAVE WE LEARNED?

Take a few moments to think about what we have learned and accomplished in this book. Sometimes, I grab a book like this and read it very quickly because I just want to get to the end. You want to see how it all goes, and then you are at the end and have not done any of the exercises; you have not started a Journal, let alone written anything down in it. The effectiveness of this book comes from the activities and the cooperative nature of the tasks. I can lead the dance, but if you do not dance too, nothing happens.

Reflect on what you have learned. If you need to, scan back and go through the exercises, drills, and reflection questions again. If you been very proactive and interactive, this book might have taken you a few weeks to finish. If you read something twenty days ago, you might not remember it that well, so it is worth taking a moment, scanning back to the chapter titles and taking a quick look through.

Here's a recap of what we have covered, to help you reflect and identify the chapters you might need to work on again.

In chapter one (Let's Talk About Stress, Baby), we defined what stress is and started identifying the sources of stress in your life using your Conquer Stress Journal.

In chapter two (How Prevalent is Stress in Your Life?), we learned about the strong prevalence of stress in many people's lives. We talked about how this is a reality we all need to face, and that there are tools that you can use to do this successfully.

Chapter three was about Negative Reactions to Stress. We went through a list of some common negative reactions to stress and reflected on which ones we can relate to. Have you identified and reflected on how to change your negative coping strategies?

In chapter four (Dealing with Stress in a Positive Way), we talked about positive ways to cope with stress with plenty of examples. Again, we reflected on our life and identified the ones we can implement to reduce our stress levels.

In chapter five (What Impact Can Stress Have on Your Life?), we went on to discuss how badly stress can affect your life if you do not choose to use positive strategies to deal with it.

And then in chapter six, we discussed Social Pressure and Stress; people can allow unnecessary stress to be put on them by deciding to buy things they cannot afford and do not need (or maybe even want) or by trying to be different just to be accepted.

In chapter seven (Reducing the Stress Level of Your Lifestyle), we went on to discuss ways you can reduce the stress level of your lifestyle. This involved making a differentiation between necessary and unnecessary sources of stress.

In chapter eight (Stress and Health), we talked about how stress can affect your physical health and reflected on the benefits of meditation.

In chapter nine (Short Case Studies), we put some of our new knowledge to work in thinking about short case studies and scenarios.

And then finally, in chapter ten (Building Your Self-Confidence), we discussed the significant place of self-confidence in our stress-effect-fighting arsenal.

If you feel that you cannot remember the content of some of the chapters, think about going back for review. The knowledge you will gain and solidify in your mind is very useful and well worth the effort!

We've now come to the end of our book on conquering stress and anxiety. I hope that you have learned a great deal and now feel more confident in your ability to combat the effects of stress on your life, health, and psychological well-being.

I recommend keeping this book as a reference. Whenever you feel stressed or maybe a little rusty on some of the things you learned, turn to this book for a refresher course! It's also a good idea to keep your Conquer Stress Journal; it will remind you of all the work you did in reading and reflecting on this book.

12

YOU MADE IT!

You are at the end this is the end of this book, and you have accomplished the goal! As I mentioned before, it takes two to tango; this is a cooperative venture. I want you to succeed and conquer your stress. I write books for a living, but I also want to make a difference; I want to affect my readers in a positive way.

In a moment, if you are reading this on Kindle, Amazon is going to ask you to leave a review of this book. But you cannot review this book unless you have interacted with me. If you are sitting there thinking, "These drills seem dumb, I am not doing these dumb exercises. I am going to leave him a one-star review," that is dishonest because you didn't even try. If you went through this book and you did the activities but they did not work, then you should absolutely leave me a bad review; I deserve it. If I let you down, if I failed you, you should tell me.

You can also let me know by emailing me. I value your honesty, and I want to make a difference for you. If you email me, I am going to write you back. I respond to every single email.

I will write you back and suggest some other things we can try or other resources and techniques you can use. I care about you solving a problem and breaking through the stress barrier. That really makes a difference.

If you found this book valuable, then I would like to interact with you more and more. I encourage you to join my Facebook group and communicate with other people that are on a similar journey to you. My Facebook group is for writers, entrepreneurs, and people who work for themselves; it is filled with people that, just like you, are dealing with stress, depression, procrastination, and all the other vagaries of life. You can surround yourself with a group of people who will encourage you and help you break through those barriers, understanding how they implemented procrastination and stress-reducing and depression-conquering techniques and succeeded.

We like to work together, and I want you to join our community. We can have a two-way conversation. This book is only the start of our conversation; this is not a monologue. My first statement is now ending; it is your opportunity to speak back to me, and I do want to hear from you.

I know what it is like to have crippling stress, and I know what it is like to be in the emergency room; you feel like you are at death's door.

When I was working with a business partner who sent me to the emergency room, the first thing he said when I came out was, "Is your little panic attack going to affect our business?" This guy was a monster; I had to cut him out of my life. He ended up stealing a great deal of money because stealing my health was not enough for him.

This was seven years ago. I ran into him when I was in America this year for three days. He looked forty years older than he is, and I felt amazing. I never did anything to him, I never pursued him, but it turned out the guy who made stress a big part of his life and nearly killed me with stress had karma give it all back to him.

This is why I do not worry about vengeance; I have faith in the universe. The only thing you need to worry about is *you*. If there are people in your life that are causing you stress, put a little distance between you and them. If you do not have the right job, it is okay to look at changing your career.

These are all little things to think about, and of course, before you make major decisions, you can talk to me and the group. You have a community of people who are very supportive and share their stories. It is a safe place, and I cannot wait to see you there. Thank you so much for trusting me enough to read this book.

As you have more questions, as you seek more guidance, and as you continue this journey, I want to be there with you. I want to see your successes, so I look forward to hearing about your positive results and achievements as you conquer stress.

MORE INFORMATION

T hroughout this book I mentioned other books, images, links, research, and additional content. All of that can be found at:

https://servenomaster.com/stress

You don't have to worry about trying to remember any other links or the names of anything mentioned in this book. Just enjoy the journey and focus on taking control of your destiny.

LET'S SOAR TOGETHER

The hardest part of dealing with stress is going it alone. When you are in isolation, the night can seem so dark. Please join my FREE, private Facebook group filled with supportive people on the same path.

https://servenomaster.com/tribal

This is a great place to chat with me daily, share your experiences with the exercises and find a supportive group of people who are all on the same journey as you.

FOUND A TYPO?

While every effort goes into ensuring that this book is flawless, it is inevitable that a mistake or two will slip through the cracks.

If you find an error of any kind in this book, please let me know by visiting:

ServeNoMaster.com/typos

I appreciate you taking the time to notify me. This ensures that future readers never have to experience that awful typo. You are making the world a better place.

ABOUT THE AUTHOR

Born in Los Angeles, raised in Nashville, educated in London - Jonathan Green has spent years wandering the globe as his own boss - but it didn't come without a price. Like most people, he struggled through years of working in a vast, unfeeling bureaucracy. And even though he was 'totally crushed' when he got fired, it gave him the chance to reappraise his life and rebuild it from scratch.

Since 2010, he's been making a full-time living on the Internet - helping brick and mortar business owners promote themselves on the Internet, helping men and women find true love, ghostwriting best sellers for some of the biggest publishers in the world and much, much more.

Thanks to smart planning and personal discipline, he was more successful than he could have possibly expected. He traveled the world, helped friends and family, and moved to an island in the South Pacific.

Now he's passing his knowledge onto the rest of the world as host of a weekly podcast that teaches financial independence, networking with the world's most influential people, writing epic stuff online, and traveling the world for cheap.

His hobbies include kayaking, surfing, and building empires. He currently has a loving girlfriend, and two wonderful kids who love the ocean (almost!) as much as he does.

Find out more about Jonathan at:
ServeNoMaster.com

BOOKS BY JONATHAN GREEN

Non-Fiction

Serve No Master Series

Serve No Master

Serve No Master (French)

Breaking Orbit

20K a Day

Control Your Fate

Break Through (coming soon)

Habit of Success Series

PROCRASTINATION

Influence and Persuasion

Overcome Depression

Stop Worrying and Anxiety

Love Yourself

Conquer Stress

Law of Attraction

Mindfulness and Meditation Ultimate Guide

Meditation Techniques for Beginners

Social Anxiety and Shyness Ultimate Guide

Coloring Depression Away with Adult Coloring Books

Don't be Quiet

Seven Secrets

Seven Networking Secrets for Jobseekers

Biographies

The Fate of my Father

Complex Adult Coloring Books

The Dinosaur Adult Coloring Book

The Dog Adult Coloring Book

The Celtic Adult Coloring Book

The Outer Space Adult Coloring Book

Irreverent Coloring Books

Dragons Are Bastards

Fiction

Gunpowder and Magic

The Outlier (As Drake Blackstone)

ONE LAST THING

Reviews are the lifeblood of any book on Amazon and especially for the independent author. If you would click five stars on your Kindle device or visit this special link at your convenience, that will ensure that I can continue to produce more books. A quick rating or review helps me to support my family and I deeply appreciate it.

Without stars and reviews, you would never have found this book. Please take just thirty seconds of your time to support an independent author by leaving a rating.

Thank you so much!

To leave a review go to ->

https://servenomaster.com/stressreview

Sincerely,

Jonathan Green

ServeNoMaster.com

Printed in Great Britain
by Amazon